THE COMEDY OF ERRORS

WILLIAM SHAKESPEARE

Published by True Sign Publishing House
Address: SY. No. 21/2 & 21/3, Sonnenahalli,
Krishnarajapura, Bengaluru,
Karnataka - 560049 India
E-mail: truesignbooks@gmail.com
Website: www.truesign.in

The Comedy of Errors
Author: William Shakespeare

ISBN: 978-93-5462-726-2

First Edition: 2022

Contents

Dramatis Personæ

SOLINUS	Duke of Ephesus.
EGEON	a Merchant of Syracuse.
ANTIPHOLUS OF EPHESUS	Twin brothers and sons to Egeon and
ANTIPHOLUS OF SYRACUSE	Emilia, but unknown to each other.
DROMIO OF EPHESUS	Twin brothers, and attendants on
DROMIO OF SYRACUSE	the two Antipholuses.
BALTHASAR	a Merchant.
ANGELO	a Goldsmith.
A MERCHANT	friend to Antipholus of Syracuse
PINCH	a Schoolmaster and a Conjurer.
EMILIA	Wife to Egeon, an Abbess at Ephesus.
ADRIANA	Wife to Antipholus of Ephesus.
LUCIANA	her Sister.
LUCE	her Servant.
A COURTESAN	Messenger, Jailer, Officers, Attendants

SCENE: Ephesus

ACT-I
SCENE-I — A hall in the Duke's palace

Enter DUKE, EGEON, JAILER, OFFICERS *and other* ATTENDANTS.

EGEON — Proceed, Solinus, to procure my fall,
And by the doom of death end woes and all.

DUKE — Merchant of Syracusa, plead no more.
I am not partial to infringe our laws.
The enmity and discord which of late
Sprung from the rancorous outrage of your Duke
To merchants, our well-dealing countrymen,
Who, wanting guilders to redeem their lives,
Have seal'd his rigorous statutes with their bloods,
Excludes all pity from our threat'ning looks.
For since the mortal and intestine jars
'Twixt thy seditious countrymen and us,
It hath in solemn synods been decreed,
Both by the Syracusians and ourselves,
To admit no traffic to our adverse towns;
Nay more, if any born at Ephesus
Be seen at Syracusian marts and fairs;
Again, if any Syracusian born
Come to the bay of Ephesus, he dies,
His goods confiscate to the Duke's dispose,
Unless a thousand marks be levied
To quit the penalty and to ransom him.
Thy substance, valued at the highest rate,
Cannot amount unto a hundred marks;
Therefore by law thou art condemn'd to die.

EGEON — Yet this my comfort; when your words are done,
My woes end likewise with the evening sun.

DUKE

Well, Syracusian, say in brief the cause
Why thou departedst from thy native home,
And for what cause thou cam'st to Ephesus.

EGEON

A heavier task could not have been impos'd
Than I to speak my griefs unspeakable;
Yet, that the world may witness that my end
Was wrought by nature, not by vile offence,
I'll utter what my sorrow gives me leave.
In Syracusa was I born, and wed
Unto a woman happy but for me,
And by me, had not our hap been bad.
With her I liv'd in joy; our wealth increas'd
By prosperous voyages I often made
To Epidamnum, till my factor's death,
And the great care of goods at random left,
Drew me from kind embracements of my spouse;
From whom my absence was not six months old
Before herself (almost at fainting under
The pleasing punishment that women bear)
Had made provision for her following me,
And soon and safe arrived where I was.
There had she not been long but she became
A joyful mother of two goodly sons,
And, which was strange, the one so like the other
As could not be distinguish'd but by names.
That very hour, and in the self-same inn,
A mean woman was delivered
Of such a burden, male twins, both alike.
Those, for their parents were exceeding poor,
I bought, and brought up to attend my sons.
My wife, not meanly proud of two such boys,
Made daily motions for our home return.
Unwilling I agreed; alas, too soon
We came aboard.
A league from Epidamnum had we sail'd
Before the always-wind-obeying deep
Gave any tragic instance of our harm;
But longer did we not retain much hope;
For what obscured light the heavens did grant
Did but convey unto our fearful minds

A doubtful warrant of immediate death,
Which though myself would gladly have embrac'd,
Yet the incessant weepings of my wife,
Weeping before for what she saw must come,
And piteous plainings of the pretty babes,
That mourn'd for fashion, ignorant what to fear,
Forc'd me to seek delays for them and me.
And this it was (for other means was none).
The sailors sought for safety by our boat,
And left the ship, then sinking-ripe, to us.
My wife, more careful for the latter-born,
Had fast'ned him unto a small spare mast,
Such as sea-faring men provide for storms.
To him one of the other twins was bound,
Whilst I had been like heedful of the other.
The children thus dispos'd, my wife and I,
Fixing our eyes on whom our care was fix'd,
Fast'ned ourselves at either end the mast,
And, floating straight, obedient to the stream,
Was carried towards Corinth, as we thought.
At length the sun, gazing upon the earth,
Dispers'd those vapours that offended us,
And by the benefit of his wished light
The seas wax'd calm, and we discovered
Two ships from far, making amain to us,
Of Corinth that, of Epidaurus this.
But ere they came—O, let me say no more!
Gather the sequel by that went before.

DUKE
Nay, forward, old man, do not break off so,
For we may pity, though not pardon thee.

EGEON
O, had the gods done so, I had not now
Worthily term'd them merciless to us.
For, ere the ships could meet by twice five leagues,
We were encountered by a mighty rock,
Which being violently borne upon,
Our helpful ship was splitted in the midst;
So that, in this unjust divorce of us,
Fortune had left to both of us alike
What to delight in, what to sorrow for.
Her part, poor soul, seeming as burdened

With lesser weight, but not with lesser woe,
Was carried with more speed before the wind,
And in our sight they three were taken up
By fishermen of Corinth, as we thought.
At length another ship had seiz'd on us;
And, knowing whom it was their hap to save,
Gave healthful welcome to their ship-wrack'd guests,
And would have reft the fishers of their prey,
Had not their bark been very slow of sail;
And therefore homeward did they bend their course.
Thus have you heard me sever'd from my bliss,
That by misfortunes was my life prolong'd
To tell sad stories of my own mishaps.

DUKE

And for the sake of them thou sorrowest for,
Do me the favour to dilate at full
What have befall'n of them and thee till now.

EGEON

My youngest boy, and yet my eldest care,
At eighteen years became inquisitive
After his brother, and importun'd me
That his attendant, so his case was like,
Reft of his brother, but retain'd his name,
Might bear him company in the quest of him;
Whom whilst I laboured of a love to see,
I hazarded the loss of whom I lov'd.
Five summers have I spent in farthest Greece,
Roaming clean through the bounds of Asia,
And, coasting homeward, came to Ephesus,
Hopeless to find, yet loath to leave unsought
Or that or any place that harbours men.
But here must end the story of my life;
And happy were I in my timely death,
Could all my travels warrant me they live.

DUKE

Hapless Egeon, whom the fates have mark'd
To bear the extremity of dire mishap;
Now, trust me, were it not against our laws,
Against my crown, my oath, my dignity,
Which princes, would they, may not disannul,
My soul should sue as advocate for thee.
But though thou art adjudged to the death,

And passed sentence may not be recall'd
But to our honour's great disparagement,
Yet will I favour thee in what I can.
Therefore, merchant, I'll limit thee this day
To seek thy health by beneficial help.
Try all the friends thou hast in Ephesus;
Beg thou, or borrow, to make up the sum,
And live; if no, then thou art doom'd to die.
Jailer, take him to thy custody.

JAILER I will, my lord.

EGEON Hopeless and helpless doth Egeon wend,
But to procrastinate his lifeless end.

[*Exeunt.*]

SCENE-II — A public place

Enter ANTIPHOLUS *and* DROMIO OF SYRACUSE *and a* MERCHANT.

MERCHANT

Therefore give out you are of Epidamnum,
Lest that your goods too soon be confiscate.
This very day a Syracusian merchant
Is apprehended for arrival here,
And, not being able to buy out his life,
According to the statute of the town
Dies ere the weary sun set in the west.
There is your money that I had to keep.

ANTIPHOLUS OF SYRACUSE

Go bear it to the Centaur, where we host,
And stay there, Dromio, till I come to thee.
Within this hour it will be dinnertime;
Till that, I'll view the manners of the town,
Peruse the traders, gaze upon the buildings,
And then return and sleep within mine inn,
For with long travel I am stiff and weary.
Get thee away.

DROMIO OF SYRACUSE

Many a man would take you at your word,
And go indeed, having so good a mean.

[*Exit* DROMIO.]

ANTIPHOLUS OF SYRACUSE A trusty villain, sir, that very oft,
When I am dull with care and melancholy,
Lightens my humour with his merry jests.
What, will you walk with me about the town,
And then go to my inn and dine with me?

MERCHANT I am invited, sir, to certain merchants,
Of whom I hope to make much benefit.
I crave your pardon. Soon, at five o'clock,
Please you, I'll meet with you upon the mart,
And afterward consort you till bedtime.
My present business calls me from you now.

ANTIPHOLUS OF SYRACUSE Farewell till then: I will go lose myself,
And wander up and down to view the city.

MERCHANT Sir, I commend you to your own content.

[*Exit* MERCHANT.]

ANTIPHOLUS OF SYRACUSE He that commends me to mine own content
Commends me to the thing I cannot get.
I to the world am like a drop of water
That in the ocean seeks another drop,
Who, failing there to find his fellow forth,
Unseen, inquisitive, confounds himself.
So I, to find a mother and a brother,
In quest of them, unhappy, lose myself.

Enter DROMIO OF EPHESUS.

Here comes the almanac of my true date.
What now? How chance thou art return'd so soon?

DROMIO OF EPHESUS
Return'd so soon? rather approach'd too late.
The capon burns, the pig falls from the spit;
The clock hath strucken twelve upon the bell;
My mistress made it one upon my cheek.
She is so hot because the meat is cold;
The meat is cold because you come not home;
You come not home because you have no stomach;
You have no stomach, having broke your fast;
But we that know what 'tis to fast and pray,
Are penitent for your default today.

ANTIPHOLUS OF SYRACUSE
Stop in your wind, sir, tell me this, I pray:
Where have you left the money that I gave you?

DROMIO OF EPHESUS
O, sixpence that I had o' Wednesday last
To pay the saddler for my mistress' crupper:
The saddler had it, sir, I kept it not.

ANTIPHOLUS OF SYRACUSE
I am not in a sportive humour now.
Tell me, and dally not, where is the money?
We being strangers here, how dar'st thou trust
So great a charge from thine own custody?

DROMIO OF EPHESUS	I pray you jest, sir, as you sit at dinner: I from my mistress come to you in post; If I return, I shall be post indeed, For she will score your fault upon my pate. Methinks your maw, like mine, should be your clock, And strike you home without a messenger.
ANTIPHOLUS OF SYRACUSE	Come, Dromio, come, these jests are out of season, Reserve them till a merrier hour than this. Where is the gold I gave in charge to thee?
DROMIO OF EPHESUS	To me, sir? why, you gave no gold to me!
ANTIPHOLUS OF SYRACUSE	Come on, sir knave, have done your foolishness, And tell me how thou hast dispos'd thy charge.
DROMIO OF EPHESUS	My charge was but to fetch you from the mart Home to your house, the Phoenix, sir, to dinner. My mistress and her sister stay for you.
ANTIPHOLUS OF SYRACUSE	Now, as I am a Christian, answer me In what safe place you have bestow'd my money, Or I shall break that merry sconce of yours That stands on tricks when I am undispos'd; Where is the thousand marks thou hadst of me?
DROMIO OF EPHESUS	I have some marks of yours upon my pate,

Some of my mistress' marks upon my shoulders,
But not a thousand marks between you both.
If I should pay your worship those again,
Perchance you will not bear them patiently.

ANTIPHOLUS OF SYRACUSE

Thy mistress' marks? what mistress, slave, hast thou?

DROMIO OF EPHESUS.

Your worship's wife, my mistress at the Phoenix;
She that doth fast till you come home to dinner,
And prays that you will hie you home to dinner.

ANTIPHOLUS OF SYRACUSE

What, wilt thou flout me thus unto my face,
Being forbid? There, take you that, sir knave.

DROMIO OF EPHESUS

What mean you, sir? for God's sake hold your hands.
Nay, an you will not, sir, I'll take my heels.

[*Exit Dromio.*]

ANTIPHOLUS OF SYRACUSE

Upon my life, by some device or other
The villain is o'er-raught of all my money.
They say this town is full of cozenage,
As nimble jugglers that deceive the eye,
Dark-working sorcerers that change the mind,
Soul-killing witches that deform the body,
Disguised cheaters, prating mountebanks,
And many such-like liberties of sin:

If it prove so, I will be gone the sooner.
I'll to the Centaur to go seek this slave.
I greatly fear my money is not safe.

[*Exit.*]

ACT-II
SCENE-I — A public place

Enter ADRIANA, *wife to* ANTIPHOLUS *(of Ephesus) with* LUCIANA *her sister.*

ADRIANA	Neither my husband nor the slave return'd That in such haste I sent to seek his master? Sure, Luciana, it is two o'clock.
LUCIANA	Perhaps some merchant hath invited him, And from the mart he's somewhere gone to dinner. Good sister, let us dine, and never fret; A man is master of his liberty; Time is their master, and when they see time, They'll go or come. If so, be patient, sister.
ADRIANA	Why should their liberty than ours be more?
LUCIANA	Because their business still lies out o' door.
ADRIANA	Look when I serve him so, he takes it ill.
LUCIANA	O, know he is the bridle of your will.
ADRIANA	There's none but asses will be bridled so.
LUCIANA	Why, headstrong liberty is lash'd with woe. There's nothing situate under heaven's eye But hath his bound in earth, in sea, in sky. The beasts, the fishes, and the winged fowls Are their males' subjects, and at their controls. Man, more divine, the masters of all these, Lord of the wide world and wild wat'ry seas,

Indued with intellectual sense and souls,
Of more pre-eminence than fish and fowls,
Are masters to their females, and their lords:
Then let your will attend on their accords.

ADRIANA This servitude makes you to keep unwed.

LUCIANA Not this, but troubles of the marriage-bed.

ADRIANA But, were you wedded, you would bear some sway.

LUCIANA Ere I learn love, I'll practise to obey.

ADRIANA How if your husband start some other where?

LUCIANA Till he come home again, I would forbear.

ADRIANA Patience unmov'd! No marvel though she pause;
They can be meek that have no other cause.
A wretched soul bruis'd with adversity,
We bid be quiet when we hear it cry;
But were we burd'ned with like weight of pain,
As much, or more, we should ourselves complain:
So thou, that hast no unkind mate to grieve thee,
With urging helpless patience would relieve me:
But if thou live to see like right bereft,
This fool-begg'd patience in thee will be left.

LUCIANA Well, I will marry one day, but to try.
Here comes your man, now is your husband nigh.

Enter DROMIO OF EPHESUS.

ADRIANA Say, is your tardy master now at hand?

DROMIO OF EPHESUS Nay, he's at two hands with me, and that my two ears can witness.

ADRIANA Say, didst thou speak with him? know'st thou his mind?

DROMIO OF EPHESUS Ay, ay, he told his mind upon mine ear.
Beshrew his hand, I scarce could understand it.

LUCIANA Spake he so doubtfully thou couldst not feel his meaning?

DROMIO OF EPHESUS Nay, he struck so plainly I could too well feel his blows; and withal so doubtfully that I could scarce understand them.

ADRIANA But say, I prithee, is he coming home?
It seems he hath great care to please his wife.

DROMIO OF EPHESUS Why, mistress, sure my master is horn-mad.

ADRIANA Horn-mad, thou villain?

DROMIO OF EPHESUS I mean not cuckold-mad,
But sure he's stark mad.
When I desir'd him to come home to dinner,
He ask'd me for a thousand marks in gold.
"'Tis dinner time," quoth I. "My gold," quoth he.
"Your meat doth burn" quoth I. "My gold," quoth he.
"Will you come home?" quoth I. "My gold," quoth he.
"Where is the thousand marks I gave thee, villain?"
"The pig" quoth I "is burn'd". "My gold," quoth he.
"My mistress, sir," quoth I. "Hang up thy mistress;
I know not thy mistress; out on thy mistress!"

LUCIANA Quoth who?

DROMIO OF EPHESUS Quoth my master.
"I know," quoth he, "no house, no wife, no mistress."
So that my errand, due unto my tongue,

I thank him, I bare home upon my shoulders;
For, in conclusion, he did beat me there.

ADRIANA
Go back again, thou slave, and fetch him home.

DROMIO OF EPHESUS
Go back again, and be new beaten home?
For God's sake, send some other messenger.

ADRIANA
Back slave, or I will break thy pate across.

DROMIO OF EPHESUS
And he will bless that cross with other beating.
Between you I shall have a holy head.

ADRIANA
Hence, prating peasant. Fetch thy master home.

DROMIO OF EPHESUS
Am I so round with you, as you with me,
That like a football you do spurn me thus?
You spurn me hence, and he will spurn me hither.
If I last in this service, you must case me in leather.

[*Exit.*]

LUCIANA
Fie, how impatience loureth in your face.

ADRIANA
His company must do his minions grace,
Whilst I at home starve for a merry look.
Hath homely age th' alluring beauty took
From my poor cheek? then he hath wasted it.
Are my discourses dull? barren my wit?
If voluble and sharp discourse be marr'd,
Unkindness blunts it more than marble hard.
Do their gay vestments his affections bait?
That's not my fault; he's master of my state.
What ruins are in me that can be found
By him not ruin'd? Then is he the ground
Of my defeatures. My decayed fair
A sunny look of his would soon repair;

But, too unruly deer, he breaks the pale
And feeds from home; poor I am but his stale.

LUCIANA Self-harming jealousy! fie, beat it hence.

ADRIANA Unfeeling fools can with such wrongs dispense.
I know his eye doth homage otherwhere,
Or else what lets it but he would be here?
Sister, you know he promis'd me a chain;
Would that alone, a love he would detain,
So he would keep fair quarter with his bed.
I see the jewel best enamelled
Will lose his beauty; yet the gold bides still
That others touch, yet often touching will
Wear gold; and no man that hath a name
By falsehood and corruption doth it shame.
Since that my beauty cannot please his eye,
I'll weep what's left away, and weeping die.

LUCIANA How many fond fools serve mad jealousy!

[*Exeunt.*]

SCENE-II — The same

Enter ANTIPHOLUS OF SYRACUSE.

ANTIPHOLUS OF SYRACUSE The gold I gave to Dromio is laid up
Safe at the Centaur, and the heedful slave
Is wander'd forth in care to seek me out.
By computation and mine host's report.
I could not speak with Dromio since at first
I sent him from the mart. See, here he comes.

Enter DROMIO OF SYRACUSE.

How now, sir! is your merry humour alter'd?
As you love strokes, so jest with me again.
You know no Centaur? you receiv'd no gold?
Your mistress sent to have me home to dinner?
My house was at the Phoenix? Wast thou mad,
That thus so madly thou didst answer me?

DROMIO OF SYRACUSE What answer, sir? when spake I such a word?

ANTIPHOLUS OF SYRACUSE Even now, even here, not half an hour since.

DROMIO OF SYRACUSE I did not see you since you sent me hence,
Home to the Centaur with the gold you gave me.

ANTIPHOLUS OF SYRACUSE Villain, thou didst deny the gold's receipt,
And told'st me of a mistress and a dinner,
For which I hope thou felt'st I was displeas'd.

DROMIO OF SYRACUSE I am glad to see you in this merry vein.
What means this jest, I pray you, master, tell me?

ANTIPHOLUS OF SYRACUSE Yea, dost thou jeer and flout me in the teeth?
Think'st thou I jest? Hold, take thou that, and that.

[*Beats* DROMIO.]

DROMIO OF SYRACUSE Hold, sir, for God's sake, now your jest is earnest.
Upon what bargain do you give it me?

ANTIPHOLUS OF SYRACUSE Because that I familiarly sometimes
Do use you for my fool, and chat with you,
Your sauciness will jest upon my love,
And make a common of my serious hours.
When the sun shines let foolish gnats make sport,
But creep in crannies when he hides his beams.
If you will jest with me, know my aspect,
And fashion your demeanour to my looks,
Or I will beat this method in your sconce.

DROMIO OF SYRACUSE	Sconce, call you it? so you would leave battering, I had rather have it a head. And you use these blows long, I must get a sconce for my head, and ensconce it too, or else I shall seek my wit in my shoulders. But I pray, sir, why am I beaten?
ANTIPHOLUS OF SYRACUSE	Dost thou not know?
DROMIO OF SYRACUSE	Nothing, sir, but that I am beaten.
ANTIPHOLUS OF SYRACUSE	Shall I tell you why?
DROMIO OF SYRACUSE	Ay, sir, and wherefore; for they say, every why hath a wherefore.
ANTIPHOLUS OF SYRACUSE	Why, first, for flouting me; and then wherefore, For urging it the second time to me.
DROMIO OF SYRACUSE	Was there ever any man thus beaten out of season, When in the why and the wherefore is neither rhyme nor reason? Well, sir, I thank you.
ANTIPHOLUS OF SYRACUSE	Thank me, sir, for what?
DROMIO OF SYRACUSE	Marry, sir, for this something that you gave me for nothing.
ANTIPHOLUS OF SYRACUSE	I'll make you amends next, to give you nothing for something. But say, sir, is it dinner-time?
DROMIO OF SYRACUSE	No, sir; I think the meat wants that I have.
ANTIPHOLUS OF SYRACUSE	In good time, sir, what's that?
DROMIO OF SYRACUSE	Basting.
ANTIPHOLUS OF SYRACUSE	Well, sir, then 'twill be dry.
DROMIO OF SYRACUSE	If it be, sir, I pray you eat none of it.
ANTIPHOLUS OF SYRACUSE	Your reason?
DROMIO OF SYRACUSE	Lest it make you choleric, and purchase me another dry basting.

ANTIPHOLUS OF SYRACUSE	Well, sir, learn to jest in good time. There's a time for all things.
DROMIO OF SYRACUSE	I durst have denied that before you were so choleric.
ANTIPHOLUS OF SYRACUSE	By what rule, sir?
DROMIO OF SYRACUSE	Marry, sir, by a rule as plain as the plain bald pate of Father Time himself.
ANTIPHOLUS OF SYRACUSE	Let's hear it.
DROMIO OF SYRACUSE	There's no time for a man to recover his hair that grows bald by nature.
ANTIPHOLUS OF SYRACUSE	May he not do it by fine and recovery?
DROMIO OF SYRACUSE	Yes, to pay a fine for a periwig, and recover the lost hair of another man.
ANTIPHOLUS OF SYRACUSE	Why is Time such a niggard of hair, being, as it is, so plentiful an excrement?
DROMIO OF SYRACUSE	Because it is a blessing that he bestows on beasts, and what he hath scanted men in hair he hath given them in wit.
ANTIPHOLUS OF SYRACUSE	Why, but there's many a man hath more hair than wit.
DROMIO OF SYRACUSE	Not a man of those but he hath the wit to lose his hair.
ANTIPHOLUS OF SYRACUSE	Why, thou didst conclude hairy men plain dealers without wit.
DROMIO OF SYRACUSE	The plainer dealer, the sooner lost. Yet he loseth it in a kind of jollity.
ANTIPHOLUS OF SYRACUSE	For what reason?
DROMIO OF SYRACUSE	For two, and sound ones too.
ANTIPHOLUS OF SYRACUSE	Nay, not sound, I pray you.
DROMIO OF SYRACUSE	Sure ones, then.
ANTIPHOLUS OF SYRACUSE	Nay, not sure, in a thing falsing.
DROMIO OF SYRACUSE	Certain ones, then.
ANTIPHOLUS OF SYRACUSE	Name them.

DROMIO OF SYRACUSE The one, to save the money that he spends in tiring; the other, that at dinner they should not drop in his porridge.

ANTIPHOLUS OF SYRACUSE You would all this time have proved there is no time for all things.

DROMIO OF SYRACUSE Marry, and did, sir; namely, e'en no time to recover hair lost by nature.

ANTIPHOLUS OF SYRACUSE But your reason was not substantial why there is no time to recover.

DROMIO OF SYRACUSE Thus I mend it: Time himself is bald, and therefore, to the world's end will have bald followers.

ANTIPHOLUS OF SYRACUSE I knew 'twould be a bald conclusion.
But soft! who wafts us yonder?

Enter ADRIANA *and* LUCIANA.

ADRIANA Ay, ay, Antipholus, look strange and frown,
Some other mistress hath thy sweet aspects.
I am not Adriana, nor thy wife.
The time was once when thou unurg'd wouldst vow
That never words were music to thine ear,
That never object pleasing in thine eye,
That never touch well welcome to thy hand,
That never meat sweet-savour'd in thy taste,
Unless I spake, or look'd, or touch'd, or carv'd to thee.
How comes it now, my husband, O, how comes it,
That thou art then estranged from thyself?
Thyself I call it, being strange to me,

That, undividable, incorporate,
Am better than thy dear self's better part.
Ah, do not tear away thyself from me;
For know, my love, as easy mayst thou fall
A drop of water in the breaking gulf,
And take unmingled thence that drop again
Without addition or diminishing,
As take from me thyself, and not me too.
How dearly would it touch thee to the quick,
Should'st thou but hear I were licentious?
And that this body, consecrate to thee,
By ruffian lust should be contaminate?
Wouldst thou not spit at me, and spurn at me,
And hurl the name of husband in my face,
And tear the stain'd skin off my harlot brow,
And from my false hand cut the wedding-ring,
And break it with a deep-divorcing vow?
I know thou canst; and therefore, see thou do it.
I am possess'd with an adulterate blot;
My blood is mingled with the crime of lust;
For if we two be one, and thou play false,
I do digest the poison of thy flesh,
Being strumpeted by thy contagion.
Keep then fair league and truce with thy true bed,
I live distain'd, thou undishonoured.

ANTIPHOLUS OF SYRACUSE	Plead you to me, fair dame? I know you not. In Ephesus I am but two hours old, As strange unto your town as to your talk, Who, every word by all my wit being scann'd, Wants wit in all one word to understand.
LUCIANA	Fie, brother, how the world is chang'd with you. When were you wont to use my sister thus? She sent for you by Dromio home to dinner.
ANTIPHOLUS OF SYRACUSE	By Dromio?
DROMIO OF SYRACUSE	By me?
ADRIANA	By thee; and this thou didst return from him, That he did buffet thee, and in his blows Denied my house for his, me for his wife.
ANTIPHOLUS OF SYRACUSE	Did you converse, sir, with this gentlewoman? What is the course and drift of your compact?
DROMIO OF SYRACUSE	I, sir? I never saw her till this time.
ANTIPHOLUS OF SYRACUSE	Villain, thou liest, for even her very words Didst thou deliver to me on the mart.
DROMIO OF SYRACUSE	I never spake with her in all my life.
ANTIPHOLUS OF SYRACUSE	How can she thus, then, call us by our names? Unless it be by inspiration.
ADRIANA	How ill agrees it with your gravity To counterfeit thus grossly with your slave,

	Abetting him to thwart me in my mood; Be it my wrong, you are from me exempt, But wrong not that wrong with a more contempt. Come, I will fasten on this sleeve of thine. Thou art an elm, my husband, I a vine, Whose weakness, married to thy stronger state, Makes me with thy strength to communicate: If aught possess thee from me, it is dross, Usurping ivy, brier, or idle moss, Who all, for want of pruning, with intrusion Infect thy sap, and live on thy confusion.
ANTIPHOLUS OF SYRACUSE	To me she speaks; she moves me for her theme. What, was I married to her in my dream? Or sleep I now, and think I hear all this? What error drives our eyes and ears amiss? Until I know this sure uncertainty I'll entertain the offer'd fallacy.
LUCIANA	Dromio, go bid the servants spread for dinner.
DROMIO OF SYRACUSE	O, for my beads! I cross me for a sinner. This is the fairy land; O spite of spites! We talk with goblins, owls, and sprites; If we obey them not, this will ensue: They'll suck our breath, or pinch us black and blue.

LUCIANA
Why prat'st thou to thyself, and answer'st not?
Dromio, thou drone, thou snail, thou slug, thou sot.

DROMIO OF SYRACUSE
I am transformed, master, am I not?

ANTIPHOLUS OF SYRACUSE
I think thou art in mind, and so am I.

DROMIO OF SYRACUSE
Nay, master, both in mind and in my shape.

ANTIPHOLUS OF SYRACUSE
Thou hast thine own form.

DROMIO OF SYRACUSE
No, I am an ape.

LUCIANA
If thou art chang'd to aught, 'tis to an ass.

DROMIO OF SYRACUSE
'Tis true; she rides me, and I long for grass.
'Tis so, I am an ass; else it could never be
But I should know her as well as she knows me.

ADRIANA
Come, come, no longer will I be a fool,
To put the finger in the eye and weep
Whilst man and master laughs my woes to scorn.
Come, sir, to dinner; Dromio, keep the gate.
Husband, I'll dine above with you today,
And shrive you of a thousand idle pranks.
Sirrah, if any ask you for your master,
Say he dines forth, and let no creature enter.
Come, sister; Dromio, play the porter well.

ANTIPHOLUS OF SYRACUSE
Am I in earth, in heaven, or in hell?
Sleeping or waking, mad, or well-advis'd?
Known unto these, and to myself disguis'd!

I'll say as they say, and persever so,
And in this mist at all adventures go.

DROMIO OF SYRACUSE — Master, shall I be porter at the gate?

ADRIANA — Ay; and let none enter, lest I break your pate.

LUCIANA — Come, come, Antipholus, we dine too late.

[*Exeunt.*]

ACT-III
SCENE-I — The same

Enter ANTIPHOLUS OF EPHESUS, *his man* DROMIO OF EPHESUS, ANGELO *the goldsmith and* BALTHASAR *the merchant.*

ANTIPHOLUS OF EPHESUS Good Signior Angelo, you must excuse us all,
My wife is shrewish when I keep not hours.
Say that I linger'd with you at your shop
To see the making of her carcanet,
And that tomorrow you will bring it home.
But here's a villain that would face me down.
He met me on the mart, and that I beat him,
And charg'd him with a thousand marks in gold,
And that I did deny my wife and house.
Thou drunkard, thou, what didst thou mean by this?

DROMIO OF EPHESUS Say what you will, sir, but I know what I know.
That you beat me at the mart I have your hand to show;
If the skin were parchment, and the blows you gave were ink,
Your own handwriting would tell you what I think.

ANTIPHOLUS OF EPHESUS I think thou art an ass.

DROMIO OF EPHESUS Marry, so it doth appear
By the wrongs I suffer and the blows I bear.
I should kick, being kick'd; and being at that pass,
You would keep from my heels, and beware of an ass.

ANTIPHOLUS OF EPHESUS You're sad, Signior Balthasar; pray God our cheer
May answer my good will and your good welcome here.

BALTHASAR I hold your dainties cheap, sir, and your welcome dear.

ANTIPHOLUS OF EPHESUS O, Signior Balthasar, either at flesh or fish
A table full of welcome makes scarce one dainty dish.

BALTHASAR Good meat, sir, is common; that every churl affords.

ANTIPHOLUS OF EPHESUS And welcome more common, for that's nothing but words.

BALTHASAR Small cheer and great welcome makes a merry feast.

ANTIPHOLUS OF EPHESUS Ay, to a niggardly host and more sparing guest.
But though my cates be mean, take them in good part;
Better cheer may you have, but not with better heart.
But soft; my door is lock'd. Go bid them let us in.

DROMIO OF EPHESUS Maud, Bridget, Marian, Cicely, Gillian, Ginn!

DROMIO OF SYRACUSE [*Within.*] Mome, malt-horse, capon, coxcomb, idiot, patch!
Either get thee from the door or sit down at the hatch:

Dost thou conjure for wenches, that thou call'st for such store
When one is one too many? Go, get thee from the door.

DROMIO OF EPHESUS — What patch is made our porter? My master stays in the street.

DROMIO OF SYRACUSE — Let him walk from whence he came, lest he catch cold on's feet.

ANTIPHOLUS OF EPHESUS — Who talks within there? Ho, open the door.

DROMIO OF SYRACUSE — Right, sir, I'll tell you when an you'll tell me wherefore.

ANTIPHOLUS OF EPHESUS — Wherefore? For my dinner. I have not dined today.

DROMIO OF SYRACUSE — Nor today here you must not; come again when you may.

ANTIPHOLUS OF EPHESUS — What art thou that keep'st me out from the house I owe?

DROMIO OF SYRACUSE — The porter for this time, sir, and my name is Dromio.

DROMIO OF EPHESUS — O villain, thou hast stolen both mine office and my name;
The one ne'er got me credit, the other mickle blame.
If thou hadst been Dromio today in my place,
Thou wouldst have chang'd thy face for a name, or thy name for an ass.

Enter LUCE *concealed from Antipholus of Ephesus and his companions.*

LUCE — [*Within.*] What a coil is there, Dromio, who are those at the gate?

DROMIO OF EPHESUS — Let my master in, Luce.

LUCE — Faith, no, he comes too late,
And so tell your master.

DROMIO OF EPHESUS — O Lord, I must laugh;
Have at you with a proverb:—Shall I set in my staff?

LUCE	Have at you with another: that's—When? can you tell?
DROMIO OF SYRACUSE	If thy name be called Luce,—Luce, thou hast answer'd him well.
ANTIPHOLUS OF EPHESUS	Do you hear, you minion? you'll let us in, I hope?
LUCE	I thought to have ask'd you.
DROMIO OF SYRACUSE	And you said no.
DROMIO OF EPHESUS	So, come, help. Well struck, there was blow for blow.
ANTIPHOLUS OF EPHESUS	Thou baggage, let me in.
LUCE	Can you tell for whose sake?
DROMIO OF EPHESUS	Master, knock the door hard.
LUCE	Let him knock till it ache.
ANTIPHOLUS OF EPHESUS	You'll cry for this, minion, if I beat the door down.
LUCE	What needs all that, and a pair of stocks in the town?

Enter ADRIANA *concealed from Antipholus of Ephesus and his companions.*

ADRIANA	[*Within.*] Who is that at the door that keeps all this noise?
DROMIO OF SYRACUSE	By my troth, your town is troubled with unruly boys.
ANTIPHOLUS OF EPHESUS	Are you there, wife? you might have come before.
ADRIANA	Your wife, sir knave? go, get you from the door.
DROMIO OF EPHESUS	If you went in pain, master, this knave would go sore.
ANGELO	Here is neither cheer, sir, nor welcome. We would fain have either.
BALTHASAR	In debating which was best, we shall part with neither.

DROMIO OF EPHESUS	They stand at the door, master; bid them welcome hither.
ANTIPHOLUS OF EPHESUS	There is something in the wind, that we cannot get in.
DROMIO OF EPHESUS	You would say so, master, if your garments were thin. Your cake here is warm within; you stand here in the cold. It would make a man mad as a buck to be so bought and sold.
ANTIPHOLUS OF EPHESUS	Go, fetch me something, I'll break ope the gate.
DROMIO OF SYRACUSE	Break any breaking here, and I'll break your knave's pate.
DROMIO OF EPHESUS	A man may break a word with you, sir, and words are but wind; Ay, and break it in your face, so he break it not behind.
DROMIO OF SYRACUSE	It seems thou want'st breaking; out upon thee, hind!
DROMIO OF EPHESUS	Here's too much "out upon thee"; I pray thee, let me in.
DROMIO OF SYRACUSE	Ay, when fowls have no feathers and fish have no fin.
ANTIPHOLUS OF EPHESUS	Well, I'll break in; go, borrow me a crow.
DROMIO OF EPHESUS	A crow without feather; master, mean you so? For a fish without a fin, there's a fowl without a feather. If a crow help us in, sirrah, we'll pluck a crow together.
ANTIPHOLUS OF EPHESUS	Go, get thee gone; fetch me an iron crow.
BALTHASAR	Have patience, sir. O, let it not be so: Herein you war against your reputation,

And draw within the compass of suspect
The unviolated honour of your wife.
Once this,—your long experience of her wisdom,
Her sober virtue, years, and modesty,
Plead on her part some cause to you unknown;
And doubt not, sir, but she will well excuse
Why at this time the doors are made against you.
Be rul'd by me; depart in patience,
And let us to the Tiger all to dinner,
And about evening, come yourself alone
To know the reason of this strange restraint.
If by strong hand you offer to break in
Now in the stirring passage of the day,
A vulgar comment will be made of it;
And that supposed by the common rout
Against your yet ungalled estimation
That may with foul intrusion enter in,
And dwell upon your grave when you are dead;
For slander lives upon succession,
For ever hous'd where it gets possession.

ANTIPHOLUS OF EPHESUS

You have prevail'd. I will depart in quiet,
And, in despite of mirth, mean to be merry.
I know a wench of excellent discourse,
Pretty and witty; wild, and yet, too, gentle;
There will we dine. This woman that I mean,

	My wife (but, I protest, without desert) Hath oftentimes upbraided me withal; To her will we to dinner.—Get you home And fetch the chain, by this I know 'tis made. Bring it, I pray you, to the Porpentine, For there's the house. That chain will I bestow (Be it for nothing but to spite my wife) Upon mine hostess there. Good sir, make haste. Since mine own doors refuse to entertain me, I'll knock elsewhere, to see if they'll disdain me.
ANGELO	I'll meet you at that place some hour hence.
ANTIPHOLUS OF EPHESUS	Do so; this jest shall cost me some expense.

[*Exeunt.*]

SCENE-II — The same

Enter LUCIANA *with* ANTIPHOLUS OF SYRACUSE.

LUCIANA

And may it be that you have quite forgot
A husband's office? Shall, Antipholus,
Even in the spring of love, thy love-springs rot?
Shall love, in building, grow so ruinous?
If you did wed my sister for her wealth,
Then for her wealth's sake use her with more kindness;
Or if you like elsewhere, do it by stealth,
Muffle your false love with some show of blindness.
Let not my sister read it in your eye;
Be not thy tongue thy own shame's orator;
Look sweet, speak fair, become disloyalty;
Apparel vice like virtue's harbinger;
Bear a fair presence though your heart be tainted;
Teach sin the carriage of a holy saint,
Be secret-false. What need she be acquainted?
What simple thief brags of his own attaint?
'Tis double wrong to truant with your bed

And let her read it in thy looks at board.
Shame hath a bastard fame, well managed;
Ill deeds is doubled with an evil word.
Alas, poor women, make us but believe,
Being compact of credit, that you love us.
Though others have the arm, show us the sleeve;
We in your motion turn, and you may move us.
Then, gentle brother, get you in again;
Comfort my sister, cheer her, call her wife.
'Tis holy sport to be a little vain
When the sweet breath of flattery conquers strife.

ANTIPHOLUS OF SYRACUSE

Sweet mistress, what your name is else, I know not,
Nor by what wonder you do hit on mine;
Less in your knowledge and your grace you show not
Than our earth's wonder, more than earth divine.
Teach me, dear creature, how to think and speak;
Lay open to my earthy gross conceit,
Smother'd in errors, feeble, shallow, weak,
The folded meaning of your words' deceit.
Against my soul's pure truth why labour you
To make it wander in an unknown field?

Are you a god? would you create me new?
Transform me, then, and to your power I'll yield.
But if that I am I, then well I know
Your weeping sister is no wife of mine,
Nor to her bed no homage do I owe.
Far more, far more, to you do I decline.
O, train me not, sweet mermaid, with thy note
To drown me in thy sister's flood of tears.
Sing, siren, for thyself, and I will dote;
Spread o'er the silver waves thy golden hairs,
And as a bed I'll take thee, and there lie,
And, in that glorious supposition think
He gains by death that hath such means to die.
Let love, being light, be drowned if she sink!

LUCIANA
What, are you mad, that you do reason so?

ANTIPHOLUS OF SYRACUSE
Not mad, but mated; how, I do not know.

LUCIANA
It is a fault that springeth from your eye.

ANTIPHOLUS OF SYRACUSE
For gazing on your beams, fair sun, being by.

LUCIANA
Gaze where you should, and that will clear your sight.

ANTIPHOLUS OF SYRACUSE
As good to wink, sweet love, as look on night.

LUCIANA
Why call you me love? Call my sister so.

ANTIPHOLUS OF SYRACUSE Thy sister's sister.

LUCIANA That's my sister.

ANTIPHOLUS OF SYRACUSE No,
It is thyself, mine own self's better part,
Mine eye's clear eye, my dear heart's dearer heart,
My food, my fortune, and my sweet hope's aim,
My sole earth's heaven, and my heaven's claim.

LUCIANA All this my sister is, or else should be.

ANTIPHOLUS OF SYRACUSE Call thyself sister, sweet, for I aim thee;
Thee will I love, and with thee lead my life;
Thou hast no husband yet, nor I no wife.
Give me thy hand.

LUCIANA O, soft, sir, hold you still;
I'll fetch my sister to get her goodwill.

[*Exit* LUCIANA.]

Enter DROMIO OF SYRACUSE.

ANTIPHOLUS OF SYRACUSE Why, how now, Dromio? where runn'st thou so fast?

DROMIO OF SYRACUSE Do you know me, sir? Am I Dromio? Am I your man? Am I myself?

ANTIPHOLUS OF SYRACUSE Thou art Dromio, thou art my man, thou art thyself.

DROMIO OF SYRACUSE I am an ass, I am a woman's man, and besides myself.

ANTIPHOLUS OF SYRACUSE What woman's man? and how besides thyself?

DROMIO OF SYRACUSE Marry, sir, besides myself, I am due to a woman, one that claims me, one that haunts me, one that will have me.

ANTIPHOLUS OF SYRACUSE What claim lays she to thee?

DROMIO OF SYRACUSE Marry, sir, such claim as you would lay to your horse, and she would have me as a beast; not that I being a beast she would have me, but that she being a very beastly creature lays claim to me.

ANTIPHOLUS OF SYRACUSE What is she?

DROMIO OF SYRACUSE A very reverent body; ay, such a one as a man may not speak of without he say "sir-reverence". I have but lean luck in the match, and yet is she a wondrous fat marriage.

ANTIPHOLUS OF SYRACUSE How dost thou mean a "fat marriage"?

DROMIO OF SYRACUSE Marry, sir, she's the kitchen wench, and all grease, and I know not what use to put her to but to make a lamp of her and run from her by her own light. I warrant her rags and the tallow in them will burn a Poland winter. If she lives till doomsday, she'll burn a week longer than the whole world.

ANTIPHOLUS OF SYRACUSE What complexion is she of?

DROMIO OF SYRACUSE Swart like my shoe, but her face nothing like so clean kept. For why? she sweats, a man may go overshoes in the grime of it.

ANTIPHOLUS OF SYRACUSE That's a fault that water will mend.

DROMIO OF SYRACUSE No, sir, 'tis in grain; Noah's flood could not do it.

ANTIPHOLUS OF SYRACUSE What's her name?

DROMIO OF SYRACUSE Nell, sir; but her name and three quarters, that's an ell and three quarters, will not measure her from hip to hip.

ANTIPHOLUS OF SYRACUSE Then she bears some breadth?

DROMIO OF SYRACUSE	No longer from head to foot than from hip to hip. She is spherical, like a globe. I could find out countries in her.
ANTIPHOLUS OF SYRACUSE	In what part of her body stands Ireland?
DROMIO OF SYRACUSE	Marry, sir, in her buttocks; I found it out by the bogs.
ANTIPHOLUS OF SYRACUSE	Where Scotland?
DROMIO OF SYRACUSE	I found it by the barrenness, hard in the palm of the hand.
ANTIPHOLUS OF SYRACUSE.	Where France?
DROMIO OF SYRACUSE	In her forehead; armed and reverted, making war against her hair.
ANTIPHOLUS OF SYRACUSE	Where England?
DROMIO OF SYRACUSE	I looked for the chalky cliffs, but I could find no whiteness in them. But I guess it stood in her chin, by the salt rheum that ran between France and it.
ANTIPHOLUS OF SYRACUSE	Where Spain?
DROMIO OF SYRACUSE	Faith, I saw it not; but I felt it hot in her breath.
ANTIPHOLUS OF SYRACUSE	Where America, the Indies?
DROMIO OF SYRACUSE	O, sir, upon her nose, all o'er-embellished with rubies, carbuncles, sapphires, declining their rich aspect to the hot breath of Spain, who sent whole armadoes of carracks to be ballast at her nose.
ANTIPHOLUS OF SYRACUSE	Where stood Belgia, the Netherlands?
DROMIO OF SYRACUSE	O, sir, I did not look so low. To conclude: this drudge or diviner laid claim to me, called me Dromio, swore I was assured to her, told me what privy marks I had about me, as the mark of my shoulder, the mole in my neck, the great wart on my left arm, that I, amazed, ran from

her as a witch. And, I think, if my breast had not been made of faith, and my heart of steel, she had transformed me to a curtal dog, and made me turn i' the wheel.

ANTIPHOLUS OF SYRACUSE

Go, hie thee presently, post to the road;
And if the wind blow any way from shore,
I will not harbour in this town tonight.
If any bark put forth, come to the mart,
Where I will walk till thou return to me.
If everyone knows us, and we know none,
'Tis time, I think, to trudge, pack and be gone.

DROMIO OF SYRACUSE

As from a bear a man would run for life,
So fly I from her that would be my wife.

[*Exit.*]

ANTIPHOLUS OF SYRACUSE

There's none but witches do inhabit here,
And therefore 'tis high time that I were hence.
She that doth call me husband, even my soul
Doth for a wife abhor. But her fair sister,
Possess'd with such a gentle sovereign grace,
Of such enchanting presence and discourse,
Hath almost made me traitor to myself.

But lest myself be guilty to self-wrong,
I'll stop mine ears against the mermaid's song.

Enter ANGELO *with the chain.*

ANGELO	Master Antipholus.
ANTIPHOLUS OF SYRACUSE	Ay, that's my name.
ANGELO	I know it well, sir. Lo, here is the chain; I thought to have ta'en you at the Porpentine, The chain unfinish'd made me stay thus long.
ANTIPHOLUS OF SYRACUSE	What is your will that I shall do with this?
ANGELO	What please yourself, sir; I have made it for you.
ANTIPHOLUS OF SYRACUSE	Made it for me, sir! I bespoke it not.
ANGELO	Not once, nor twice, but twenty times you have. Go home with it, and please your wife withal, And soon at supper-time I'll visit you, And then receive my money for the chain.
ANTIPHOLUS OF SYRACUSE	I pray you, sir, receive the money now, For fear you ne'er see chain nor money more.
ANGELO	You are a merry man, sir; fare you well.

[*Exit.*]

ANTIPHOLUS OF SYRACUSE	What I should think of this I cannot tell, But this I think, there's no man is so vain That would refuse so fair an offer'd chain. I see a man here needs not live by shifts,

When in the streets he meets such golden gifts.
I'll to the mart, and there for Dromio stay;
If any ship put out, then straight away.

[*Exit.*]

ACT-IV
SCENE-I — The same

Enter MERCHANT, ANGELO *and an* OFFICER.

MERCHANT

You know since Pentecost the sum is due,
And since I have not much importun'd you,
Nor now I had not, but that I am bound
To Persia, and want guilders for my voyage;
Therefore make present satisfaction,
Or I'll attach you by this officer.

ANGELO

Even just the sum that I do owe to you
Is growing to me by Antipholus,
And in the instant that I met with you
He had of me a chain; at five o'clock
I shall receive the money for the same.
Pleaseth you walk with me down to his house,
I will discharge my bond, and thank you too.

Enter ANTIPHOLUS OF EPHESUS *and* DROMIO OF EPHESUS *from the Courtesan's.*

OFFICER

That labour may you save. See where he comes.

ANTIPHOLUS OF EPHESUS

While I go to the goldsmith's house, go thou
And buy a rope's end; that will I bestow

Among my wife and her confederates
For locking me out of my doors by day.
But soft, I see the goldsmith; get thee gone;
Buy thou a rope, and bring it home to me.

DROMIO OF EPHESUS — I buy a thousand pound a year! I buy a rope!

[*Exit* DROMIO.]

ANTIPHOLUS OF EPHESUS — A man is well holp up that trusts to you,
I promised your presence and the chain,
But neither chain nor goldsmith came to me.
Belike you thought our love would last too long
If it were chain'd together, and therefore came not.

ANGELO — Saving your merry humour, here's the note
How much your chain weighs to the utmost carat,
The fineness of the gold, and chargeful fashion,
Which doth amount to three odd ducats more
Than I stand debted to this gentleman.
I pray you, see him presently discharg'd,
For he is bound to sea, and stays but for it.

ANTIPHOLUS OF EPHESUS — I am not furnished with the present money;
Besides, I have some business in the town.
Good signior, take the stranger to my house,

	And with you take the chain, and bid my wife Disburse the sum on the receipt thereof; Perchance I will be there as soon as you.
ANGELO	Then you will bring the chain to her yourself.
ANTIPHOLUS OF EPHESUS	No, bear it with you, lest I come not time enough.
ANGELO	Well, sir, I will. Have you the chain about you?
ANTIPHOLUS OF EPHESUS	And if I have not, sir, I hope you have, Or else you may return without your money.
ANGELO	Nay, come, I pray you, sir, give me the chain; Both wind and tide stays for this gentleman, And I, to blame, have held him here too long.
ANTIPHOLUS OF EPHESUS	Good Lord, you use this dalliance to excuse Your breach of promise to the Porpentine. I should have chid you for not bringing it, But, like a shrew, you first begin to brawl.
MERCHANT	The hour steals on; I pray you, sir, dispatch.
ANGELO	You hear how he importunes me. The chain!
ANTIPHOLUS OF EPHESUS	Why, give it to my wife, and fetch your money.
ANGELO	Come, come, you know I gave it you even now.

	Either send the chain or send by me some token.
ANTIPHOLUS OF EPHESUS	Fie, now you run this humour out of breath. Come, where's the chain? I pray you, let me see it.
MERCHANT	My business cannot brook this dalliance. Good sir, say whe'er you'll answer me or no; If not, I'll leave him to the officer.
ANTIPHOLUS OF EPHESUS	I answer you? What should I answer you?
ANGELO	The money that you owe me for the chain.
ANTIPHOLUS OF EPHESUS	I owe you none till I receive the chain.
ANGELO	You know I gave it you half an hour since.
ANTIPHOLUS OF EPHESUS	You gave me none. You wrong me much to say so.
ANGELO	You wrong me more, sir, in denying it. Consider how it stands upon my credit.
MERCHANT	Well, officer, arrest him at my suit.
OFFICER	I do, and charge you in the duke's name to obey me.
ANGELO	This touches me in reputation. Either consent to pay this sum for me, Or I attach you by this officer.
ANTIPHOLUS OF EPHESUS	Consent to pay thee that I never had? Arrest me, foolish fellow, if thou dar'st.
ANGELO	Here is thy fee; arrest him, officer. I would not spare my brother in this case If he should scorn me so apparently.
OFFICER	I do arrest you, sir. You hear the suit.

ANTIPHOLUS OF EPHESUS — I do obey thee till I give thee bail.
But, sirrah, you shall buy this sport as dear
As all the metal in your shop will answer.

ANGELO — Sir, sir, I shall have law in Ephesus,
To your notorious shame, I doubt it not.

Enter DROMIO OF SYRACUSE *from the bay.*

DROMIO OF SYRACUSE — Master, there's a bark of Epidamnum
That stays but till her owner comes aboard,
And then, sir, bears away. Our fraughtage, sir,
I have convey'd aboard, and I have bought
The oil, the balsamum, and aqua-vitae.
The ship is in her trim; the merry wind
Blows fair from land; they stay for nought at all
But for their owner, master, and yourself.

ANTIPHOLUS OF EPHESUS — How now? a madman? Why, thou peevish sheep,
What ship of Epidamnum stays for me?

DROMIO OF SYRACUSE — A ship you sent me to, to hire waftage.

ANTIPHOLUS OF EPHESUS — Thou drunken slave, I sent thee for a rope,
And told thee to what purpose and what end.

DROMIO OF SYRACUSE — You sent me for a rope's end as soon.
You sent me to the bay, sir, for a bark.

ANTIPHOLUS OF EPHESUS — I will debate this matter at more leisure,
And teach your ears to list me with more heed.
To Adriana, villain, hie thee straight:

Give her this key, and tell her in the desk
That's cover'd o'er with Turkish tapestry
There is a purse of ducats; let her send it.
Tell her I am arrested in the street,
And that shall bail me. Hie thee, slave; be gone.
On, officer, to prison till it come.

[*Exeunt* MERCHANT, ANGELO, OFFICER *and* ANTIPHOLUS OF EPHESUS.]

DROMIO OF SYRACUSE

To Adriana, that is where we din'd,
Where Dowsabel did claim me for her husband.
She is too big, I hope, for me to compass.
Thither I must, although against my will,
For servants must their masters' minds fulfil.

[*Exit.*]

SCENE-II — The same

Enter ADRIANA *and* LUCIANA.

ADRIANA Ah, Luciana, did he tempt thee so?
Might'st thou perceive austerely in his eye
That he did plead in earnest, yea or no?
Look'd he or red or pale, or sad or merrily?
What observation mad'st thou in this case
Of his heart's meteors tilting in his face?

LUCIANA First he denied you had in him no right.

ADRIANA He meant he did me none; the more my spite.

LUCIANA Then swore he that he was a stranger here.

ADRIANA And true he swore, though yet forsworn he were.

LUCIANA Then pleaded I for you.

ADRIANA And what said he?

LUCIANA That love I begg'd for you he begg'd of me.

ADRIANA With what persuasion did he tempt thy love?

LUCIANA With words that in an honest suit might move.
First he did praise my beauty, then my speech.

ADRIANA Did'st speak him fair?

LUCIANA Have patience, I beseech.

ADRIANA I cannot, nor I will not hold me still.
My tongue, though not my heart, shall have his will.
He is deformed, crooked, old, and sere,
Ill-fac'd, worse bodied, shapeless everywhere;
Vicious, ungentle, foolish, blunt, unkind,
Stigmatical in making, worse in mind.

LUCIANA Who would be jealous then of such a one?
No evil lost is wail'd when it is gone.

ADRIANA — Ah, but I think him better than I say,
And yet would herein others' eyes were worse:
Far from her nest the lapwing cries away;
My heart prays for him, though my tongue do curse.

Enter DROMIO OF SYRACUSE.

DROMIO OF SYRACUSE — Here, go; the desk, the purse, sweet now, make haste.

LUCIANA — How hast thou lost thy breath?

DROMIO OF SYRACUSE — By running fast.

ADRIANA — Where is thy master, Dromio? is he well?

DROMIO OF SYRACUSE — No, he's in Tartar limbo, worse than hell.
A devil in an everlasting garment hath him,
One whose hard heart is button'd up with steel;
A fiend, a fairy, pitiless and rough;
A wolf, nay worse, a fellow all in buff;
A back-friend, a shoulder-clapper, one that countermands
The passages of alleys, creeks, and narrow lands;
A hound that runs counter, and yet draws dryfoot well,
One that, before the judgment, carries poor souls to hell.

ADRIANA — Why, man, what is the matter?

DROMIO OF SYRACUSE — I do not know the matter. He is 'rested on the case.

ADRIANA — What, is he arrested? Tell me at whose suit?

DROMIO OF SYRACUSE — I know not at whose suit he is arrested, well;

But he's in a suit of buff which 'rested him, that can I tell.
Will you send him, mistress, redemption, the money in his desk?

ADRIANA Go fetch it, sister. This I wonder at,

[*Exit* LUCIANA.]

Thus he unknown to me should be in debt.
Tell me, was he arrested on a band?

DROMIO OF SYRACUSE Not on a band, but on a stronger thing;
A chain, a chain. Do you not hear it ring?

ADRIANA What, the chain?

DROMIO OF SYRACUSE No, no, the bell, 'tis time that I were gone.
It was two ere I left him, and now the clock strikes one.

ADRIANA The hours come back! That did I never hear.

DROMIO OF SYRACUSE O yes, if any hour meet a sergeant, 'a turns back for very fear.

ADRIANA As if time were in debt. How fondly dost thou reason!

DROMIO OF SYRACUSE Time is a very bankrupt, and owes more than he's worth to season.
Nay, he's a thief too. Have you not heard men say
That time comes stealing on by night and day?
If he be in debt and theft, and a sergeant in the way,
Hath he not reason to turn back an hour in a day?

Enter LUCIANA.

ADRIANA Go, Dromio, there's the money, bear it straight,

And bring thy master home immediately.
Come, sister, I am press'd down with conceit;
Conceit, my comfort and my injury.

[*Exeunt.*]

SCENE-III — The same

Enter ANTIPHOLUS OF SYRACUSE.

ANTIPHOLUS OF SYRACUSE There's not a man I meet but doth salute me
As if I were their well-acquainted friend,
And everyone doth call me by my name.
Some tender money to me, some invite me;
Some other give me thanks for kindnesses;
Some offer me commodities to buy.
Even now a tailor call'd me in his shop,
And show'd me silks that he had bought for me,
And therewithal took measure of my body.
Sure, these are but imaginary wiles,
And Lapland sorcerers inhabit here.

Enter DROMIO OF SYRACUSE.

DROMIO OF SYRACUSE Master, here's the gold you sent me for.
What, have you got the picture of old Adam new apparelled?

ANTIPHOLUS OF SYRACUSE What gold is this? What Adam dost thou mean?

DROMIO OF SYRACUSE Not that Adam that kept the paradise, but that Adam that keeps the prison; he that goes in the calf's skin that was killed for the Prodigal; he that came behind you, sir, like an evil angel, and bid you forsake your liberty.

ANTIPHOLUS OF SYRACUSE — I understand thee not.

DROMIO OF SYRACUSE — No? Why, 'tis a plain case: he that went like a bass-viol in a case of leather; the man, sir, that, when gentlemen are tired, gives them a sob, and 'rests them; he, sir, that takes pity on decayed men and gives them suits of durance; he that sets up his rest to do more exploits with his mace than a morris-pike.

ANTIPHOLUS OF SYRACUSE — What! thou mean'st an officer?

DROMIO OF SYRACUSE — Ay, sir, the sergeant of the band; he that brings any man to answer it that breaks his band; one that thinks a man always going to bed, and says, "God give you good rest."

ANTIPHOLUS OF SYRACUSE — Well, sir, there rest in your foolery. Is there any ship puts forth tonight? may we be gone?

DROMIO OF SYRACUSE — Why, sir, I brought you word an hour since that the bark *Expedition* put forth tonight, and then were you hindered by the sergeant to tarry for the hoy *Delay*. Here are the angels that you sent for to deliver you.

ANTIPHOLUS OF SYRACUSE — The fellow is distract, and so am I,
And here we wander in illusions.
Some blessed power deliver us from hence!

Enter a COURTESAN.

COURTESAN — Well met, well met, Master Antipholus.
I see, sir, you have found the goldsmith now.
Is that the chain you promis'd me today?

ANTIPHOLUS OF SYRACUSE Satan, avoid! I charge thee, tempt me not.

DROMIO OF SYRACUSE Master, is this Mistress Satan?

ANTIPHOLUS OF SYRACUSE It is the devil.

DROMIO OF SYRACUSE Nay, she is worse, she is the devil's dam; and here she comes in the habit of a light wench, and thereof comes that the wenches say "God damn me", that's as much to say, "God make me a light wench." It is written they appear to men like angels of light. Light is an effect of fire, and fire will burn; ergo, light wenches will burn. Come not near her.

COURTESAN Your man and you are marvellous merry, sir.
Will you go with me? We'll mend our dinner here.

DROMIO OF SYRACUSE Master, if you do, expect spoon-meat, or bespeak a long spoon.

ANTIPHOLUS OF SYRACUSE Why, Dromio?

DROMIO OF SYRACUSE Marry, he must have a long spoon that must eat with the devil.

ANTIPHOLUS OF SYRACUSE Avoid then, fiend! What tell'st thou me of supping?
Thou art, as you are all, a sorceress.
I conjure thee to leave me and be gone.

COURTESAN Give me the ring of mine you had at dinner,
Or, for my diamond, the chain you promis'd,
And I'll be gone, sir, and not trouble you.

DROMIO OF SYRACUSE Some devils ask but the paring of one's nail,
A rush, a hair, a drop of blood, a pin,
A nut, a cherry-stone; but she, more covetous,
Would have a chain.

Master, be wise; and if you give it her,
The devil will shake her chain and fright us with it.

COURTESAN — I pray you, sir, my ring, or else the chain;
I hope you do not mean to cheat me so.

ANTIPHOLUS OF SYRACUSE — Avaunt, thou witch! Come, Dromio, let us go.

DROMIO OF SYRACUSE — Fly pride, says the peacock. Mistress, that you know.

[*Exeunt* ANTIPHOLUS OF SYRACUSE *and* DROMIO OF SYRACUSE.]

COURTESAN — Now, out of doubt Antipholus is mad,
Else would he never so demean himself.
A ring he hath of mine worth forty ducats,
And for the same he promis'd me a chain;
Both one and other he denies me now.
The reason that I gather he is mad,
Besides this present instance of his rage,
Is a mad tale he told today at dinner
Of his own doors being shut against his entrance.
Belike his wife, acquainted with his fits,
On purpose shut the doors against his way.
My way is now to hie home to his house,
And tell his wife that, being lunatic,
He rush'd into my house and took perforce
My ring away. This course I fittest choose,
For forty ducats is too much to lose.

[*Exit.*]

SCENE-IV — The same

Enter ANTIPHOLUS OF EPHESUS *with an* OFFICER.

ANTIPHOLUS OF EPHESUS	Fear me not, man, I will not break away: I'll give thee ere I leave thee so much money, To warrant thee, as I am 'rested for. My wife is in a wayward mood today, And will not lightly trust the messenger That I should be attach'd in Ephesus; I tell you 'twill sound harshly in her ears.

Enter DROMIO OF EPHESUS *with a rope's end.*

	Here comes my man. I think he brings the money. How now, sir! have you that I sent you for?
DROMIO OF EPHESUS	Here's that, I warrant you, will pay them all.
ANTIPHOLUS OF EPHESUS	But where's the money?
DROMIO OF EPHESUS	Why, sir, I gave the money for the rope.
ANTIPHOLUS OF EPHESUS	Five hundred ducats, villain, for a rope?
DROMIO OF EPHESUS	I'll serve you, sir, five hundred at the rate.
ANTIPHOLUS OF EPHESUS	To what end did I bid thee hie thee home?
DROMIO OF EPHESUS	To a rope's end, sir; and to that end am I return'd.

ANTIPHOLUS OF EPHESUS — And to that end, sir, I will welcome you.

[*Beating him.*]

OFFICER — Good sir, be patient.

DROMIO OF EPHESUS — Nay, 'tis for me to be patient. I am in adversity.

OFFICER — Good now, hold thy tongue.

DROMIO OF EPHESUS — Nay, rather persuade him to hold his hands.

ANTIPHOLUS OF EPHESUS — Thou whoreson, senseless villain.

DROMIO OF EPHESUS — I would I were senseless, sir, that I might not feel your blows.

ANTIPHOLUS OF EPHESUS — Thou art sensible in nothing but blows, and so is an ass.

DROMIO OF EPHESUS — I am an ass indeed; you may prove it by my long ears. I have served him from the hour of my nativity to this instant, and have nothing at his hands for my service but blows. When I am cold, he heats me with beating; when I am warm he cools me with beating. I am waked with it when I sleep, raised with it when I sit, driven out of doors with it when I go from home, welcomed home with it when I return. Nay, I bear it on my shoulders as a beggar wont her brat; and I think when he hath lamed me, I shall beg with it from door to door.

Enter ADRIANA, LUCIANA, COURTESAN *and a* SCHOOLMASTER *called* PINCH.

ANTIPHOLUS OF EPHESUS — Come, go along, my wife is coming yonder.

DROMIO OF EPHESUS — Mistress, *respice finem*, respect your end, or rather, the prophesy like the parrot, "Beware the rope's end."

ANTIPHOLUS OF EPHESUS — Wilt thou still talk?

[*Beats him.*]

COURTESAN How say you now? Is not your husband mad?

ADRIANA His incivility confirms no less.
Good Doctor Pinch, you are a conjurer;
Establish him in his true sense again,
And I will please you what you will demand.

LUCIANA Alas, how fiery and how sharp he looks!

COURTESAN Mark how he trembles in his ecstasy.

PINCH Give me your hand, and let me feel your pulse.

ANTIPHOLUS OF EPHESUS There is my hand, and let it feel your ear.

PINCH I charge thee, Satan, hous'd within this man,
To yield possession to my holy prayers,
And to thy state of darkness hie thee straight.
I conjure thee by all the saints in heaven.

ANTIPHOLUS OF EPHESUS Peace, doting wizard, peace; I am not mad.

ADRIANA O, that thou wert not, poor distressed soul!

ANTIPHOLUS OF EPHESUS You minion, you, are these your customers?
Did this companion with the saffron face
Revel and feast it at my house today,
Whilst upon me the guilty doors were shut,
And I denied to enter in my house?

ADRIANA O husband, God doth know you din'd at home,
Where would you had remain'd until this time,

	Free from these slanders and this open shame.
ANTIPHOLUS OF EPHESUS	Din'd at home? Thou villain, what sayest thou?
DROMIO OF EPHESUS	Sir, sooth to say, you did not dine at home.
ANTIPHOLUS OF EPHESUS	Were not my doors lock'd up and I shut out?
DROMIO OF EPHESUS	Perdy, your doors were lock'd, and you shut out.
ANTIPHOLUS OF EPHESUS	And did not she herself revile me there?
DROMIO OF EPHESUS	Sans fable, she herself revil'd you there.
ANTIPHOLUS OF EPHESUS	Did not her kitchen-maid rail, taunt, and scorn me?
DROMIO OF EPHESUS	Certes, she did, the kitchen-vestal scorn'd you.
ANTIPHOLUS OF EPHESUS	And did not I in rage depart from thence?
DROMIO OF EPHESUS	In verity, you did; my bones bear witness, That since have felt the vigour of his rage.
ADRIANA	Is't good to soothe him in these contraries?
PINCH	It is no shame; the fellow finds his vein, And yielding to him, humours well his frenzy.
ANTIPHOLUS OF EPHESUS	Thou hast suborn'd the goldsmith to arrest me.
ADRIANA	Alas! I sent you money to redeem you By Dromio here, who came in haste for it.
DROMIO OF EPHESUS	Money by me? Heart and goodwill you might, But surely, master, not a rag of money.

ANTIPHOLUS OF EPHESUS	Went'st not thou to her for a purse of ducats?
ADRIANA	He came to me, and I deliver'd it.
LUCIANA	And I am witness with her that she did.
DROMIO OF EPHESUS	God and the rope-maker bear me witness That I was sent for nothing but a rope.
PINCH	Mistress, both man and master is possess'd, I know it by their pale and deadly looks. They must be bound and laid in some dark room.
ANTIPHOLUS OF EPHESUS	Say, wherefore didst thou lock me forth today, And why dost thou deny the bag of gold?
ADRIANA	I did not, gentle husband, lock thee forth.
DROMIO OF EPHESUS	And gentle master, I receiv'd no gold; But I confess, sir, that we were lock'd out.
ADRIANA	Dissembling villain, thou speak'st false in both.
ANTIPHOLUS OF EPHESUS	Dissembling harlot, thou art false in all, And art confederate with a damned pack To make a loathsome abject scorn of me. But with these nails I'll pluck out these false eyes That would behold in me this shameful sport.

[*Enter three or four, and offer to bind him. He strives.*]

ADRIANA	O, bind him, bind him; let him not come near me.

PINCH	More company; the fiend is strong within him.
LUCIANA	Ay me, poor man, how pale and wan he looks!
ANTIPHOLUS OF EPHESUS	What, will you murder me? Thou jailer, thou, I am thy prisoner. Wilt thou suffer them To make a rescue?
OFFICER	Masters, let him go. He is my prisoner, and you shall not have him.
PINCH	Go, bind this man, for he is frantic too.
ADRIANA	What wilt thou do, thou peevish officer? Hast thou delight to see a wretched man Do outrage and displeasure to himself?
OFFICER	He is my prisoner. If I let him go, The debt he owes will be requir'd of me.
ADRIANA	I will discharge thee ere I go from thee; Bear me forthwith unto his creditor, And knowing how the debt grows, I will pay it. Good master doctor, see him safe convey'd Home to my house. O most unhappy day!
ANTIPHOLUS OF EPHESUS	O most unhappy strumpet!
DROMIO OF EPHESUS	Master, I am here enter'd in bond for you.
ANTIPHOLUS OF EPHESUS	Out on thee, villain! wherefore dost thou mad me?
DROMIO OF EPHESUS	Will you be bound for nothing? Be mad, good master; cry, "the devil".

LUCIANA God help, poor souls, how idly do they talk!

ADRIANA Go bear him hence. Sister, go you with me.

[*Exeunt* PINCH *and Assistants, with* ANTIPHOLUS OF EPHESUS *and* DROMIO OF EPHESUS.]

Say now, whose suit is he arrested at?

OFFICER One Angelo, a goldsmith; do you know him?

ADRIANA I know the man. What is the sum he owes?

OFFICER Two hundred ducats.

ADRIANA Say, how grows it due?

OFFICER Due for a chain your husband had of him.

ADRIANA He did bespeak a chain for me, but had it not.

COURTESAN When as your husband, all in rage, today
Came to my house and took away my ring,
The ring I saw upon his finger now,
Straight after did I meet him with a chain.

ADRIANA It may be so, but I did never see it.
Come, jailer, bring me where the goldsmith is,
I long to know the truth hereof at large.

Enter ANTIPHOLUS OF SYRACUSE *with his* RAPIER DRAWN, *and* DROMIO OF SYRACUSE.

LUCIANA God, for thy mercy, they are loose again!

ADRIANA And come with naked swords. Let's call more help
To have them bound again.

OFFICER — Away, they'll kill us.

[*Exeunt, as fast as may be, frighted.*]

ANTIPHOLUS OF SYRACUSE — I see these witches are afraid of swords.

DROMIO OF SYRACUSE — She that would be your wife now ran from you.

ANTIPHOLUS OF SYRACUSE — Come to the Centaur, fetch our stuff from thence.
I long that we were safe and sound aboard.

DROMIO OF SYRACUSE — Faith, stay here this night, they will surely do us no harm; you saw they speak us fair, give us gold. Methinks they are such a gentle nation that, but for the mountain of mad flesh that claims marriage of me, I could find in my heart to stay here still and turn witch.

ANTIPHOLUS OF SYRACUSE — I will not stay tonight for all the town;
Therefore away, to get our stuff aboard.

[*Exeunt.*]

ACT-V
SCENE-I — The same

Enter MERCHANT *and* ANGELO.

ANGELO	I am sorry, sir, that I have hinder'd you, But I protest he had the chain of me, Though most dishonestly he doth deny it.
MERCHANT	How is the man esteem'd here in the city?
ANGELO	Of very reverend reputation, sir, Of credit infinite, highly belov'd, Second to none that lives here in the city. His word might bear my wealth at any time.
MERCHANT	Speak softly. Yonder, as I think, he walks.

Enter ANTIPHOLUS OF SYRACUSE *and* DROMIO OF SYRACUSE.

ANGELO	'Tis so; and that self chain about his neck Which he forswore most monstrously to have. Good sir, draw near to me, I'll speak to him. Signior Antipholus, I wonder much That you would put me to this shame and trouble, And not without some scandal to yourself,

With circumstance and oaths so to deny
This chain, which now you wear so openly.
Beside the charge, the shame, imprisonment,
You have done wrong to this my honest friend,
Who, but for staying on our controversy,
Had hoisted sail and put to sea today.
This chain you had of me, can you deny it?

ANTIPHOLUS OF SYRACUSE I think I had: I never did deny it.

MERCHANT Yes, that you did, sir, and forswore it too.

ANTIPHOLUS OF SYRACUSE Who heard me to deny it or forswear it?

MERCHANT These ears of mine, thou know'st, did hear thee.
Fie on thee, wretch. 'Tis pity that thou liv'st
To walk where any honest men resort.

ANTIPHOLUS OF SYRACUSE Thou art a villain to impeach me thus;
I'll prove mine honour and mine honesty
Against thee presently, if thou dar'st stand.

MERCHANT I dare, and do defy thee for a villain.

[*They draw.*]

Enter ADRIANA, LUCIANA, COURTESAN *and* OTHERS.

ADRIANA Hold, hurt him not, for God's sake, he is mad.
Some get within him, take his sword away.
Bind Dromio too, and bear them to my house.

DROMIO OF SYRACUSE — Run, master, run, for God's sake, take a house.
This is some priory; in, or we are spoil'd.

[*Exeunt* ANTIPHOLUS OF SYRACUSE *and* DROMIO OF SYRACUSE *to the priory.*]

Enter Lady ABBESS.

ABBESS — Be quiet, people. Wherefore throng you hither?

ADRIANA — To fetch my poor distracted husband hence.
Let us come in, that we may bind him fast
And bear him home for his recovery.

ANGELO — I knew he was not in his perfect wits.

MERCHANT — I am sorry now that I did draw on him.

ABBESS — How long hath this possession held the man?

ADRIANA — This week he hath been heavy, sour, sad,
And much different from the man he was.
But till this afternoon his passion
Ne'er brake into extremity of rage.

ABBESS — Hath he not lost much wealth by wreck of sea?
Buried some dear friend? Hath not else his eye
Stray'd his affection in unlawful love?
A sin prevailing much in youthful men
Who give their eyes the liberty of gazing?
Which of these sorrows is he subject to?

ADRIANA — To none of these, except it be the last,
Namely, some love that drew him oft from home.

ABBESS
You should for that have reprehended him.

ADRIANA
Why, so I did.

ABBESS
Ay, but not rough enough.

ADRIANA
As roughly as my modesty would let me.

ABBESS
Haply in private.

ADRIANA
And in assemblies too.

ABBESS
Ay, but not enough.

ADRIANA
It was the copy of our conference.
In bed he slept not for my urging it;
At board he fed not for my urging it;
Alone, it was the subject of my theme;
In company I often glanced it;
Still did I tell him it was vile and bad.

ABBESS
And thereof came it that the man was mad.
The venom clamours of a jealous woman
Poisons more deadly than a mad dog's tooth.
It seems his sleeps were hindered by thy railing,
And thereof comes it that his head is light.
Thou say'st his meat was sauc'd with thy upbraidings.
Unquiet meals make ill digestions;
Thereof the raging fire of fever bred,
And what's a fever but a fit of madness?
Thou say'st his sports were hinder'd by thy brawls.
Sweet recreation barr'd, what doth ensue
But moody and dull melancholy,
Kinsman to grim and comfortless despair,

And at her heels a huge infectious troop
Of pale distemperatures and foes to life?
In food, in sport, and life-preserving rest
To be disturb'd would mad or man or beast.
The consequence is, then, thy jealous fits
Hath scar'd thy husband from the use of's wits.

LUCIANA She never reprehended him but mildly,
When he demean'd himself rough, rude, and wildly.
Why bear you these rebukes and answer not?

ADRIANA She did betray me to my own reproof.
Good people, enter and lay hold on him.

ABBESS No, not a creature enters in my house.

ADRIANA Then let your servants bring my husband forth.

ABBESS Neither. He took this place for sanctuary,
And it shall privilege him from your hands
Till I have brought him to his wits again,
Or lose my labour in assaying it.

ADRIANA I will attend my husband, be his nurse,
Diet his sickness, for it is my office,
And will have no attorney but myself;
And therefore let me have him home with me.

ABBESS Be patient, for I will not let him stir
Till I have used the approved means I have,

With wholesome syrups, drugs, and holy prayers,
To make of him a formal man again.
It is a branch and parcel of mine oath,
A charitable duty of my order;
Therefore depart, and leave him here with me.

ADRIANA
I will not hence and leave my husband here;
And ill it doth beseem your holiness
To separate the husband and the wife.

ABBESS
Be quiet and depart. Thou shalt not have him.

[*Exit* ABBESS.]

LUCIANA
Complain unto the duke of this indignity.

ADRIANA
Come, go. I will fall prostrate at his feet,
And never rise until my tears and prayers
Have won his grace to come in person hither
And take perforce my husband from the abbess.

MERCHANT
By this, I think, the dial points at five.
Anon, I'm sure, the Duke himself in person
Comes this way to the melancholy vale,
The place of death and sorry execution
Behind the ditches of the abbey here.

ANGELO
Upon what cause?

MERCHANT
To see a reverend Syracusian merchant,
Who put unluckily into this bay
Against the laws and statutes of this town,
Beheaded publicly for his offence.

ANGELO

See where they come. We will behold his death.

LUCIANA

Kneel to the Duke before he pass the abbey.

Enter the DUKE, *attended;* EGEON, *bareheaded; with the* HEADSMAN *and other Officers.*

DUKE

Yet once again proclaim it publicly,
If any friend will pay the sum for him,
He shall not die; so much we tender him.

ADRIANA

Justice, most sacred duke, against the abbess!

DUKE

She is a virtuous and a reverend lady,
It cannot be that she hath done thee wrong.

ADRIANA

May it please your grace, Antipholus, my husband,
Who I made lord of me and all I had
At your important letters, this ill day
A most outrageous fit of madness took him;
That desp'rately he hurried through the street,
With him his bondman all as mad as he,
Doing displeasure to the citizens
By rushing in their houses, bearing thence
Rings, jewels, anything his rage did like.
Once did I get him bound and sent him home,
Whilst to take order for the wrongs I went,
That here and there his fury had committed.
Anon, I wot not by what strong escape,
He broke from those that had the guard of him,

And with his mad attendant and himself,
Each one with ireful passion, with drawn swords,
Met us again, and, madly bent on us,
Chased us away; till raising of more aid,
We came again to bind them. Then they fled
Into this abbey, whither we pursued them.
And here the abbess shuts the gates on us,
And will not suffer us to fetch him out,
Nor send him forth that we may bear him hence.
Therefore, most gracious duke, with thy command
Let him be brought forth and borne hence for help.

DUKE

Long since thy husband serv'd me in my wars,
And I to thee engag'd a prince's word,
When thou didst make him master of thy bed,
To do him all the grace and good I could.
Go, some of you, knock at the abbey gate,
And bid the lady abbess come to me.
I will determine this before I stir.

Enter a MESSENGER.

MESSENGER

O mistress, mistress, shift and save yourself.
My master and his man are both broke loose,
Beaten the maids a-row, and bound the doctor,
Whose beard they have singed off with brands of fire,

And ever as it blazed they threw on him
Great pails of puddled mire to quench the hair.
My master preaches patience to him, and the while
His man with scissors nicks him like a fool;
And sure (unless you send some present help)
Between them they will kill the conjurer.

ADRIANA

Peace, fool, thy master and his man are here,
And that is false thou dost report to us.

MESSENGER

Mistress, upon my life, I tell you true.
I have not breath'd almost since I did see it.
He cries for you, and vows, if he can take you,
To scorch your face and to disfigure you.

[*Cry within.*]

Hark, hark, I hear him, mistress. Fly, be gone!

DUKE

Come, stand by me, fear nothing. Guard with halberds.

ADRIANA

Ay me, it is my husband. Witness you
That he is borne about invisible.
Even now we hous'd him in the abbey here,
And now he's there, past thought of human reason.

Enter ANTIPHOLUS *and* DROMIO OF EPHESUS.

ANTIPHOLUS OF EPHESUS

Justice, most gracious duke; O, grant me justice!
Even for the service that long since I did thee

When I bestrid thee in the wars, and took
Deep scars to save thy life; even for the blood
That then I lost for thee, now grant me justice.

EGEON	Unless the fear of death doth make me dote, I see my son Antipholus and Dromio.
ANTIPHOLUS OF EPHESUS	Justice, sweet prince, against that woman there. She whom thou gav'st to me to be my wife; That hath abused and dishonour'd me Even in the strength and height of injury. Beyond imagination is the wrong That she this day hath shameless thrown on me.
DUKE	Discover how, and thou shalt find me just.
ANTIPHOLUS OF EPHESUS	This day, great duke, she shut the doors upon me While she with harlots feasted in my house.
DUKE	A grievous fault. Say, woman, didst thou so?
ADRIANA	No, my good lord. Myself, he, and my sister Today did dine together. So befall my soul As this is false he burdens me withal.
LUCIANA	Ne'er may I look on day nor sleep on night But she tells to your highness simple truth.
ANGELO	O perjur'd woman! They are both forsworn.

In this the madman justly chargeth them.

ANTIPHOLUS OF EPHESUS

My liege, I am advised what I say,
Neither disturb'd with the effect of wine,
Nor heady-rash, provok'd with raging ire,
Albeit my wrongs might make one wiser mad.
This woman lock'd me out this day from dinner.
That goldsmith there, were he not pack'd with her,
Could witness it, for he was with me then,
Who parted with me to go fetch a chain,
Promising to bring it to the Porpentine,
Where Balthasar and I did dine together.
Our dinner done, and he not coming thither,
I went to seek him. In the street I met him,
And in his company that gentleman.
There did this perjur'd goldsmith swear me down
That I this day of him receiv'd the chain,
Which, God he knows, I saw not. For the which
He did arrest me with an officer.
I did obey, and sent my peasant home
For certain ducats. He with none return'd.
Then fairly I bespoke the officer
To go in person with me to my house.
By th' way we met

My wife, her sister, and a rabble more
Of vile confederates. Along with them
They brought one Pinch, a hungry lean-faced villain,
A mere anatomy, a mountebank,
A threadbare juggler, and a fortune-teller;
A needy, hollow-ey'd, sharp-looking wretch;
A living dead man. This pernicious slave,
Forsooth, took on him as a conjurer,
And gazing in mine eyes, feeling my pulse,
And with no face (as 'twere) outfacing me,
Cries out, I was possess'd. Then altogether
They fell upon me, bound me, bore me thence,
And in a dark and dankish vault at home
There left me and my man, both bound together,
Till gnawing with my teeth my bonds in sunder,
I gain'd my freedom and immediately
Ran hither to your Grace, whom I beseech
To give me ample satisfaction
For these deep shames and great indignities.

ANGELO My lord, in truth, thus far I witness with him,
That he din'd not at home, but was lock'd out.

DUKE But had he such a chain of thee, or no?

ANGELO He had, my lord, and when he ran in here

	These people saw the chain about his neck.
MERCHANT	Besides, I will be sworn these ears of mine Heard you confess you had the chain of him, After you first forswore it on the mart, And thereupon I drew my sword on you; And then you fled into this abbey here, From whence I think you are come by miracle.
ANTIPHOLUS OF EPHESUS	I never came within these abbey walls, Nor ever didst thou draw thy sword on me. I never saw the chain, so help me heaven; And this is false you burden me withal.
DUKE	Why, what an intricate impeach is this! I think you all have drunk of Circe's cup. If here you hous'd him, here he would have been. If he were mad, he would not plead so coldly. You say he din'd at home, the goldsmith here Denies that saying. Sirrah, what say you?
DROMIO OF EPHESUS	Sir, he dined with her there, at the Porpentine.
COURTESAN	He did, and from my finger snatch'd that ring.
ANTIPHOLUS OF EPHESUS	'Tis true, my liege, this ring I had of her.
DUKE	Saw'st thou him enter at the abbey here?
COURTESAN	As sure, my liege, as I do see your grace.

DUKE
Why, this is strange. Go call the abbess hither.
I think you are all mated, or stark mad.

[*Exit one to the Abbess.*]

EGEON
Most mighty Duke, vouchsafe me speak a word;
Haply I see a friend will save my life
And pay the sum that may deliver me.

DUKE
Speak freely, Syracusian, what thou wilt.

EGEON
Is not your name, sir, call'd Antipholus?
And is not that your bondman Dromio?

DROMIO OF EPHESUS
Within this hour I was his bondman, sir,
But he, I thank him, gnaw'd in two my cords.
Now am I Dromio, and his man, unbound.

EGEON
I am sure you both of you remember me.

DROMIO OF EPHESUS
Ourselves we do remember, sir, by you.
For lately we were bound as you are now.
You are not Pinch's patient, are you, sir?

EGEON
Why look you strange on me? you know me well.

ANTIPHOLUS OF EPHESUS
I never saw you in my life till now.

EGEON
O! grief hath chang'd me since you saw me last,
And careful hours with time's deformed hand,
Have written strange defeatures in my face.
But tell me yet, dost thou not know my voice?

ANTIPHOLUS OF EPHESUS
Neither.

EGEON
Dromio, nor thou?

DROMIO OF EPHESUS
No, trust me, sir, nor I.

EGEON
I am sure thou dost.

DROMIO OF EPHESUS
Ay, sir, but I am sure I do not, and whatsoever a man denies, you are now bound to believe him.

EGEON
Not know my voice! O time's extremity,
Hast thou so crack'd and splitted my poor tongue
In seven short years that here my only son
Knows not my feeble key of untun'd cares?
Though now this grained face of mine be hid
In sap-consuming winter's drizzled snow,
And all the conduits of my blood froze up,
Yet hath my night of life some memory,
My wasting lamps some fading glimmer left,
My dull deaf ears a little use to hear.
All these old witnesses, I cannot err,
Tell me thou art my son Antipholus.

ANTIPHOLUS OF EPHESUS
I never saw my father in my life.

EGEON
But seven years since, in Syracusa, boy,
Thou know'st we parted; but perhaps, my son,
Thou sham'st to acknowledge me in misery.

ANTIPHOLUS OF EPHESUS
The duke and all that know me in the city,
Can witness with me that it is not so.
I ne'er saw Syracusa in my life.

DUKE I tell thee, Syracusian, twenty years
Have I been patron to Antipholus,
During which time he ne'er saw Syracusa.
I see thy age and dangers make thee dote.

Enter the ABBESS *with* ANTIPHOLUS OF SYRACUSE *and* DROMIO OF SYRACUSE.

ABBESS Most mighty duke, behold a man much wrong'd.

[*All gather to see them.*]

ADRIANA I see two husbands, or mine eyes deceive me.

DUKE One of these men is *genius* to the other;
And so of these, which is the natural man,
And which the spirit? Who deciphers them?

DROMIO OF SYRACUSE I, sir, am Dromio, command him away.

DROMIO OF EPHESUS I, sir, am Dromio, pray let me stay.

ANTIPHOLUS OF SYRACUSE Egeon, art thou not? or else his ghost?

DROMIO OF SYRACUSE O, my old master, who hath bound him here?

ABBESS Whoever bound him, I will loose his bonds,
And gain a husband by his liberty.
Speak, old Egeon, if thou be'st the man
That hadst a wife once called Emilia,
That bore thee at a burden two fair sons.
O, if thou be'st the same Egeon, speak,
And speak unto the same Emilia!

DUKE Why, here begins his morning story right:
These two Antipholus', these two so like,

	And these two Dromios, one in semblance, Besides her urging of her wreck at sea. These are the parents to these children, Which accidentally are met together.
EGEON	If I dream not, thou art Emilia. If thou art she, tell me where is that son That floated with thee on the fatal raft?
ABBESS	By men of Epidamnum, he and I And the twin Dromio, all were taken up; But, by and by, rude fishermen of Corinth By force took Dromio and my son from them, And me they left with those of Epidamnum. What then became of them I cannot tell; I to this fortune that you see me in.
DUKE	Antipholus, thou cam'st from Corinth first?
ANTIPHOLUS OF SYRACUSE	No, sir, not I, I came from Syracuse.
DUKE	Stay, stand apart, I know not which is which.
ANTIPHOLUS OF EPHESUS	I came from Corinth, my most gracious lord.
DROMIO OF EPHESUS	And I with him.
ANTIPHOLUS OF EPHESUS	Brought to this town by that most famous warrior, Duke Menaphon, your most renowned uncle.
ADRIANA	Which of you two did dine with me today?

ANTIPHOLUS OF SYRACUSE	I, gentle mistress.
ADRIANA	And are not you my husband?
ANTIPHOLUS OF EPHESUS	No, I say nay to that.
ANTIPHOLUS OF SYRACUSE	And so do I, yet did she call me so; And this fair gentlewoman, her sister here, Did call me brother. What I told you then, I hope I shall have leisure to make good, If this be not a dream I see and hear.
ANGELO	That is the chain, sir, which you had of me.
ANTIPHOLUS OF SYRACUSE	I think it be, sir. I deny it not.
ANTIPHOLUS OF EPHESUS	And you, sir, for this chain arrested me.
ANGELO	I think I did, sir. I deny it not.
ADRIANA	I sent you money, sir, to be your bail By Dromio, but I think he brought it not.
DROMIO OF EPHESUS	No, none by me.
ANTIPHOLUS OF SYRACUSE	This purse of ducats I receiv'd from you, And Dromio my man did bring them me. I see we still did meet each other's man, And I was ta'en for him, and he for me, And thereupon these errors are arose.
ANTIPHOLUS OF EPHESUS	These ducats pawn I for my father here.
DUKE	It shall not need, thy father hath his life.
COURTESAN	Sir, I must have that diamond from you.
ANTIPHOLUS OF EPHESUS	There, take it, and much thanks for my good cheer.

ABBESS — Renowned duke, vouchsafe to take the pains
To go with us into the abbey here,
And hear at large discoursed all our fortunes;
And all that are assembled in this place,
That by this sympathised one day's error
Have suffer'd wrong, go, keep us company,
And we shall make full satisfaction.
Thirty-three years have I but gone in travail
Of you, my sons, and till this present hour
My heavy burden ne'er delivered.
The duke, my husband, and my children both,
And you, the calendars of their nativity,
Go to a gossips' feast, and go with me.
After so long grief, such nativity.

DUKE — With all my heart, I'll gossip at this feast.

[*Exeunt except the two* DROMIOS *and two Brothers.*]

DROMIO OF SYRACUSE — Master, shall I fetch your stuff from shipboard?

ANTIPHOLUS OF EPHESUS — Dromio, what stuff of mine hast thou embark'd?

DROMIO OF SYRACUSE — Your goods that lay at host, sir, in the Centaur.

ANTIPHOLUS OF SYRACUSE — He speaks to me; I am your master, Dromio.
Come, go with us. We'll look to that anon.
Embrace thy brother there, rejoice with him.

[*Exeunt* ANTIPHOLUS OF SYRACUSE *and* ANTIPHOLUS OF EPHESUS.]

DROMIO OF SYRACUSE There is a fat friend at your master's house,
That kitchen'd me for you today at dinner.
She now shall be my sister, not my wife.

DROMIO OF EPHESUS Methinks you are my glass, and not my brother.
I see by you I am a sweet-faced youth.
Will you walk in to see their gossiping?

DROMIO OF SYRACUSE Not I, sir, you are my elder.

DROMIO OF EPHESUS That's a question, how shall we try it?

DROMIO OF SYRACUSE We'll draw cuts for the senior. Till then, lead thou first.

DROMIO OF EPHESUS Nay, then, thus:
We came into the world like brother and brother,
And now let's go hand in hand, not one before another.

[*Exeunt.*]

* * *

www.ingramcontent.com/pod-product-compliance
Lightning Source LLC
LaVergne TN
LVHW101928220826
846093LV00009B/397

9789354627262